••• **Sue Ireland and Joanna Kosta**

GW01003568

Workbook

with answers

PET

DIRECT

CAMBRIDGE
UNIVERSITY PRESS

Contents

I love meeting new people

Language practice

1 Match the two halves of the sentences.

0 Sam's really good
1 Tom's not keen
2 I'm not at all interested
3 Anna's very keen
4 Ruby and Ben are really interested
5 I'd like to be better

A in going shopping. It's boring.
B on acting. She's in a drama club at school.
C at mountain biking. He's won prizes for it.
D at Maths, but it's so difficult.
E on coming to the cinema with us. He hasn't got much money.
F in music. They play in a rock band.

2 Label the pictures with these words.

acting   cycling   dancing   football   photography   windsurfing

1 _____ 2 _____ 3 _____ 4 _____ 5 _____ 6 _____

_____ _____ _____ _____ _____ _____
_____ _____ _____ _____ _____ _____
_____ _____ _____ _____ _____ _____

3 These words are all connected to the hobbies in Activity 2. Write them under the correct picture.

album   audience   ball   beach   board   brakes   camera   curtain   goal
helmet   music   partner   pictures   pitch   sail   stage   steps   wheels

4 Text and email messages between friends often use letters, numbers and short forms of words which sound like the full form of the word. For example:

b = be	b4 = before	u = you	pls = please	2 = to, too	thnx = thanks
c = see	gr8 = great	y = why	l8r = later	4 = for	wot = what
r = are	cd = could				

c u l8r

What does the message on the phone say? _____

5 Can you work out what these messages mean? Write the full forms.

0 hi how ru?

  Hi, how are you? _____

1 y rnt u speaking 2 me?

  _____

2 ru ok?

  _____

3 pls send me a msg b4 2nite

  _____

4 thnx 4 a gr8 party

  _____

5 cd u call me 2moro @ 11?

  _____

1.2 Keeping in touch

Language practice

1 Match the words to make six compound nouns connected with computers.

0	web		A	board
1	key		B	mat
2	lap		C	saver
3	mouse		D	site
4	pass		E	top
5	screen		F	word

2 Use the words in Activity 1 to complete these sentences.

0 I found a great _website_ called Minijunk.com – it's got lots of fun games on it.

1 Dad often does work on his _____ on the train.

2 Oh no! I've forgotten my _____ . I'll have to think of a new one before I can use this site.

3 After Sam spilled a cup of coffee over the _____ of his computer, several of the letters didn't work.

4 This really cool _____ appears on my computer if I don't type anything for 60 seconds.

5 When I registered at college I got this free _____ with a picture of the college on it. It's horrible!

3 Choose the correct words to complete the email.

To:	Colin
≡▼ Subject:	Swimming

Hi Colin

Sorry, I'd like to come swimming with you but I **(0) help /** am helping Dad in the garden today. Why not come to dinner with us on Sunday instead? We usually **(1) have / are having** our meal at midday at weekends, but at the moment we **(2) eat / are eating** later because it's so hot. We can have a barbecue!

By the way, I **(3) use / am using** my sister's mobile because mine **(4) needs / is needing** a new battery. Give me a call – you **(5) know / are knowing** the number, don't you?

Josh

Exam practice: Reading Part 1

4 Look at the text in each question. What does it say? Circle the correct letter A, B or C.

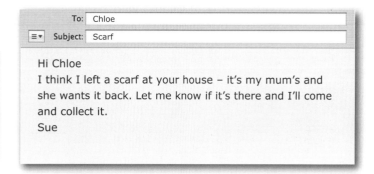

George,
I'm not going to college today. Can you ask Lisa to call me at home about tonight? My mobile's broken and I don't know her number.
Tim

To:	Chloe
≡▼ Subject:	Scarf

Hi Chloe
I think I left a scarf at your house – it's my mum's and she wants it back. Let me know if it's there and I'll come and collect it.
Sue

1 What should George do?

A give Lisa a message

B call Lisa this evening

C find Lisa's phone number

2 Sue wants Chloe to

A return the scarf to Sue's mother.

B tell her when she can collect the scarf.

C check whether she has the scarf.

2.1 He's the youngest brother

Language practice

1 Write *absolutely* or *very* in front of the adjectives.

1 My cousin bakes _absolutely_ delicious cakes. He's a(n) _____ good cook.
2 Our new teacher's _____ great. His lessons are _____ interesting.
3 We didn't have a(n) _____ pleasant holiday - the weather was _____ awful.
4 My new apartment isn't _____ close to where I work, but it's _____ enormous!

2 Match the adjectives in A to their opposites in B. Then complete the sentences with one word from each pair.

A	B
lazy	confident
mean	funny
polite	generous
sensible	hard-working
serious	rude
shy	silly

0 A person who never makes any effort is _lazy_.
1 A person who never does stupid things is _____.
2 A person who feels uncomfortable meeting new people is _____.
3 A person who makes you laugh is _____.
4 A person who dislikes spending money is _____.
5 A person who has good manners is _____.

Exam practice: Reading Part 5

3 Read the text below and choose the correct word for each space.
For each question, circle the correct letter A, B, C or D.

The Royle Family

There are six stars in this TV comedy series: parents Jim and Barbara Royle, **(0)** _their_ children Denise and Antony, Barbara's mum Nana, and Denise's husband Dave. They are **(1)** _____ of the most popular families on TV.

The programmes are always **(2)** _____ in Jim and Barbara's living room, where everyone sits on the sofa in front of the television. Jim, who hasn't **(3)** _____ a living for years, laughs at his own **(4)** _____ and is lazy and rude – **(5)** _____ to Nana. It's his hard-working wife, Barbara, who is in **(6)** _____ of things. She also defends their son Antony against the other family **(7)** _____, who seem to think he is their servant.

Daughter Denise is just as lazy **(8)** _____ her father, and she's spoilt too. She **(9)** _____ to get her husband Dave to do everything for her. **(10)** _____ both Denise and Nana have their own houses, they never seem to spend any time there.

0 A their	B his	C its	D her
1 A some	B all	C one	D many
2 A put	B kept	C set	D had
3 A earned	B worked	C employed	D managed
4 A words	B fun	C jokes	D acts
5 A really	B surely	C fairly	D especially
6 A turn	B charge	C case	D advance
7 A members	B people	C colleagues	D partners
8 A as	B like	C so	D than
9 A achieves	B persuades	C succeeds	D manages
10 A Whether	B Although	C Yet	D Despite

2.2 Such a messy room

Language practice

1 Look at the pictures and complete the puzzle. Which word appears at 1 down?

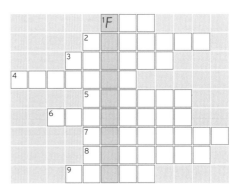

2 John is at university in London. He is staying in a student flat. Complete his email to his friend with *so*, *such*, *too* or *enough*.

To: Dave

Subject: I'm so cold!

London's OK, but I'm staying in **(0)** _____*such*_____ an awful room, it's **(1)** _____ cold I have to wear my hat and gloves all the time. The curtains are **(2)** _____ thin to keep the light out and my duvet isn't thick **(3)** _____ to keep me warm at night. There's **(4)** _____ a big gap under the door that the wind blows in and there's never **(5)** _____ hot water for a shower. And the rent is **(6)** _____ high that I can't even afford to buy an extra blanket. Thank goodness I'm moving next week!

Exam practice: Writing Part 2

3 Your family have just moved into a new apartment.
Write an email to your English friend, Billy.

In your email, you should

- tell Billy about the new apartment
- explain why you like it
- invite Billy to stay with you.

Write 35–45 words.

It used to be different

Language practice

1 An archaeologist is talking about a 5,000-year-old village discovered on a Scottish island. Complete the information using *used to / didn't use to* and one of these verbs.

build burn eat hang have keep ~~live~~ make store

The objects we have found tell us a lot about how the inhabitants of this Stone Age village (0) _used to live_ . We know they (1) _____ their houses half under the ground, to protect themselves from the terrible storms. To keep warm, they (2) _____ seaweed on the open fire. They (3) _____ their beds with dried grass and animal skins.

They (4) _____ meat in the smoky roof space of their houses. Of course they (5) _____ fridges, so they (6) _____ fish and seafood in pools of water in the floor. We know they (7) _____ chickens either, so they (8) _____ eggs they took from the nests of seabirds.

Exam practice: Reading Part 4

A journey back in time

Kentwell Hall is a large, 16th-century house built 400 years ago during the Tudor period of English history. For several weeks every summer, up to 200 actors re-create Tudor life there. Visitors to the Kentwell Re-Creation will watch people who dress, talk and do things just as they used to do them in Tudor times.

You don't have to be a professional to be in the annual Kentwell Re-Creation and you won't be paid, but anyone of any age can apply to take part. Sixteen-year-old Sally Hampton started doing it four years ago.

'There are lots of different roles. For three years I was a servant in the kitchen and learnt a lot about the food and ingredients the Tudors used, and also about the society at that time. This year I'm in a group of players who go round performing

songs and dances. Sometimes I play an original Tudor instrument, rather like a flute, and I've learnt lots of 16th-century tunes. My favourite is called Greensleeves.'

'The Kentwell Re-Creation is a fantastic opportunity to get away from the 21st century. It means leaving your mobile and your jeans behind and living like a 16th-century person. When I first started I felt a bit stupid in my costume, trying to speak old-fashioned English but I got over it very quickly because everyone else was doing the same. And I've made so many friends here, I can't wait to come back again.'

2 Read the text and questions below. For each question, circle the correct letter A, B, C or D.

1 Where would you find this text?
  A in a newspaper
  B in a history book
  C in a list of jobs for actors
  D in a travel guide

2 In her present role at the Kentwell Re-Creation, Sally
  A performs in a theatre.
  B helps to prepare food.
  C works as a waiter.
  D uses her musical skills.

3 When Sally takes part in the Kentwell Re-Creation, she
  A enjoys making people laugh.
  B is embarrassed by her costume.
  C has to talk in a special way.
  D misses modern technology.

4 What might Sally write on a postcard to a friend?

A *Come and see me at Kentwell for the day. But you must wear a Tudor costume.*

B *Why don't you apply for the Kentwell Re-Creation next year? It's fantastic fun!*

C *This will be my last time at Kentwell. Speaking old-fashioned English is just too difficult.*

D *The professional actors here get paid more than we do, but they're great to work with.*

3.2 The street is lined with trees

Language practice

1 Put the letters in the right order and label the pictures.

SCARSPERKY   FATIONNU   AMTERPANT CLOBK   MEUMUS   SULCEPURT   CALTHARED

0 _fountain_   **1** _____   **2** _____   **3** _____   **4** _____   **5** _____

2 Complete the sentences using *due to* or *owing to* and these words.

the singer's illness   fire safety rules   flooding   its position on the coast   the heavy traffic on the roads

0 This door must be kept closed _due to / owing to fire safety rules_.
1 London became a successful port _____ .
2 In winter, the road by the river often used to be closed _____ .
3 _____ , the quickest way to get around Rome is by underground.
4 _____ , the open-air concert was put off until the following week.

3 Rewrite these sentences in either the active or the passive, starting with the words given.

0 A Christmas festival was held in my city for the first time last year.
Last year they _held a Christmas festival in my city for the first time_.
1 They didn't allow traffic to come into the centre.
Traffic _____ .
2 Stalls were set up in the square by food-sellers.
Food-sellers _____ .

3 They built a skating rink in the park.
A skating rink _____ .
4 Crowds of people of all ages filled the streets.
The streets _____ .
5 Everybody who went there enjoyed the event.
The event _____ .
6 Another festival will be organised next year.
They _____ .

Exam practice: Reading Part 1

4 Look at the text in each question. What does it say? Circle the correct letter A, B or C.

1
> **Clerigos Tower**
> 225 steps!
> Unsuitable for the elderly and very young children

What is the purpose of this notice?
A to apologise
B to make a suggestion
C to give a warning

2
> **City Park**
> Take a free calendar for times and prices
> of next month's events

A Entrance to the park will be free at certain times next month.
B This will tell you what's on in the park next month.
C There will be no charge for park activities next month.

3
> **New Street Station**
> All trains are running late today
> due to a lack of staff

A There will be a delay to your journey today.
B Ask station staff for information on train times today.
C We apologise for the late arrival of your train.

4
> **Road repairs here 13–15 June**
> road will remain open, but no parking allowed

A It will not be possible to drive here for three days.
B Workmen will not finish repairing this road until 13 June.
C You cannot leave cars here between 13 and 15 June.

Let's celebrate!

4.1 Shall we have a party?

Language practice

1 Complete the puzzle with food words.
Which word do the highlighted letters spell?

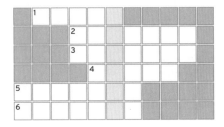

1 This is how a cake is cooked.
2 This green vegetable is very good for you.
3 This is a popular kind of ice cream.
4 This round vegetable has a strong taste and smell.
5 This is how food is cooked on a barbecue.
6 You have this after your main course.

2 Complete the emails with one of the modals. There may be more than one right answer.

should may might could

To: Hal
≡▼ Subject: Help!

Hi Hal,
Help! I've invited some friends round for my birthday party on Saturday afternoon. What **(0)** _should_ I do to make sure everyone has fun?
Tim

To: Tim
≡▼ Subject: Birthday party

Hi Tim,
Well, I think the most important thing is to buy lots of food and drink. You **(1)** _____ not need it all, but at least you won't run out. Also, you **(2)** _____ have plenty of things for people to do. Maybe you **(3)** _____ put up a volleyball net in the garden, or set up some board games in the living room. Another thing is to make sure you've got enough places for people to sit. You **(4)** _____ find that more people turn up at your party than you expected! Oh, and don't let people bring their own CDs – you **(5)** _____ not share their taste in music!
Have fun!
Hal

Exam practice: Writing Part 1

3 Here are some sentences about a woman who works as a party organiser. For each question, complete the second sentence so that it means the same as the first.

Use no more than three words.

0 Kate Elkin left school without any qualifications.
  When Kate Elkin left school, she ___*didn't*___ have any qualifications.
1 She worked in a shop that sold things for parties.
  She had a _____ in a shop that sold things for parties.
2 One day, a customer asked Kate to help her organise a party.
  One day, a customer said 'Can _____ organise a party?'
3 Kate and the woman spent several weeks planning the party.
  It took Kate and the woman several weeks _____ the party.
4 The party was so good that the woman recommended Kate to all her friends.
  It was _____ good party that the woman recommended Kate to all her friends.
5 Now Kate is the most popular party organiser in London.
  Now Kate is _____ than any other party organiser in London.

4.2 You'll be given a lot to eat!

Language practice

1 Match the adjectives to the food.

0 black coffee   A salty
1 lemons   B sweet
2 chilli sauce   C bitter
3 strawberry ice cream D hot
4 crisps   E sour

2 Complete the holiday blog with these quantifiers.

much   a few   many   a couple of   some   a little

This is a picture of me in my favourite café. It was only **(0)** ___a few___ minutes'
walk from our hotel and we spent **(1)** _____ happy evenings there - nearly
every evening, in fact! It had a really fantastic atmosphere, and the food was
delicious. **(2)** _____ times a week, usually on Fridays and Saturdays, a live
band played and everyone could dance. They had **(3)** _____ computers there
too, so I could spend **(4)** _____ time during the evening checking my emails.
I had so **(5)** _____ fun there, I'm really looking forward to going back.

Exam practice: Reading Part 3

3 Look at the sentences below about a man who owns a chain of restaurants. Read the text to decide
if each sentence is correct or incorrect. If it is correct, put a tick (✔) in the box under A for YES.
If it is not correct, put a tick (✔) in the box under B for NO.

A: YES   B: NO

1 The first 'El Rio' became a popular restaurant as soon as it opened.   ☐   ☐
2 As a teenager, Andrew Benton always had clear plans for his future.   ☐   ☐
3 Andrew worked in a number of restaurants before he turned 40.   ☐   ☐
4 Andrew's first job involved working with musicians.   ☐   ☐
5 Andrew failed in his career as a stage designer.   ☐   ☐
6 The idea of starting a restaurant came from Andrew's friend.   ☐   ☐
7 Andrew thought about opening a restaurant for many years before deciding to do it. ☐   ☐

**Andrew Benton,
restaurant owner
and businessman**

Andrew Benton opened his first 'El Rio' restaurant in 2003, selling Mexican food in a bright, modern environment. It was an immediate success and he now has a chain of restaurants across the country. All this is not bad for someone who left school at the age of 15 with no idea of what he wanted to do with his life.

He had several jobs through his 20s and 30s, but none of them had anything to do with food or cooking. In fact, he started out as a 'roadie' for a rock band. He looked after the band's instruments and sound equipment and set up the stage for them. After that, he became a stage designer. He designed sets for some very famous bands, and became well known in the industry, but he never felt satisfied with his achievements and was always thinking of other things he could do instead.

One day, he was discussing a few ideas with a friend of his, when the friend suggested he should open a restaurant. Andrew says he knew straight away that that was what he wanted to do. He went away and began doing some research, and two years later opened his first 'El Rio'. The rest is history.

How do you feel?

5.1 It's terribly painful

Language practice

1 Use the clues to complete the puzzle with parts of the body.
Which other word do the highlighted letters spell?

0 The doctor sometimes listens to this.
1 You have five of these on each foot.
2 These are between your neck and your arms.
3 You have one on each hand.
4 This is where your foot joins your leg.
5 This is at the bottom of your face.
6 This gets sore when you have a bad cough.

2 Cross out the incorrect word in each group in these sentences.

1 Moira **caught / kept / got** a cold at the weekend and now she's got a **sore / nasty / bad** cough as well.
2 She got some medicine from the chemist's, but it **smelt / looked / felt** so disgusting that she didn't **eat / take / try** it.
3 Luckily Tom wasn't **badly / heavily / seriously** hurt when he fell off his bike, although he's got a big **dressing / bandage / damage** on his knee.
4 Take one **tablet / medicine / painkiller** before you go to bed if you still have a **fever / hurt / headache**.

3 Put the first aid advice in the right order and match it to the problems below.

0 a clean dressing / You ought to / with a bandage / over the cut / tie / .
   You ought to tie a clean dressing over the cut with a bandage.   C

1 hold it / You should / under cold running water / for at least ten minutes / .

   _____   ___

2 for a few minutes / You ought to / quietly with / above your head / your feet / lie down / .

   _____   ___

3 You should / for ten minutes / firmly / the soft part of your nose / hold / .

   _____   ___

A I've burnt my arm on the oven door. **B** I'm having a nose bleed. **C** I've cut myself. **D** I feel a bit faint.

Exam practice: Writing Part 2

4 You have to hand in a piece of work today, but you had an accident and it is not finished yet.
Write an email to your teacher.

In your email, you should
• apologise
• explain why it isn't finished
• say when you will hand it in.
Write 35-45 words.

12

Language practice

1 Pablo loves the new sports centre in his town. Choose the correct words to complete his blog.

I went to the new swimming pool yesterday – it's **(1) amazed / amazing!**
The diving boards are so high they look really **(2) frightened / frightening.**
The lifeguards at the pool looked rather **(3) boring / bored** – I suppose that's because they don't find the job very **(4) interested / interesting.**
I was really **(5) surprised / surprising** when they turned the wave machine on. It's absolutely brilliant!
My little sister is very **(6) excited / exciting** about coming with me next time.

Exam practice: Reading Part 2

2 These people all want to improve their health and fitness. Read about the fitness centres below and decide which fitness centre would be the most suitable for them.

1 Paulina is a runner and recently broke a bone in her foot. She needs help with a daily exercise programme to help her improve her fitness before she starts racing again.

2 Louis and Jane would like to take their seven-year-old twin boys to a fitness centre on Saturdays and Sundays. They would all like to do a different activity.

3 Leroy works in a city office and would like to get fit by swimming regularly in his lunch hour during the week.

A Bodyspace

Forget the stress of everyday life in our ultra-modern gym and 20-metre swimming pool in the heart of the business district. Membership benefits include a free fitness check and a personal diet plan prepared by one of our friendly gym staff. There are discounts for families.

B Chestnuts Health Club

Located in the city centre, this fitness club has weights, cycles, a dance studio, steam room and sauna, making it perfect for a lunchtime workout. There is also a beauty salon and a juice bar. Membership can be for one, three or twelve months.

C Eastwick Leisure

This lively public leisure centre has over 100 very reasonably-priced activities including weekend games sessions for kids. There is a 25-metre pool (closed weekdays 9 a.m.–3.30 p.m. for local schools) plus a gym and a children's pool. For relaxation there are sunbeds and steam rooms. There's also a snack bar and a baby-care room.

D Empire Health Club

This members-only sports club has two floors of serious fitness and weight-training equipment, including boxing facilities. There is a steam room to relax in after your session. Tuesdays and Thursdays are for women only, Mondays, Wednesdays and Fridays are reserved for men.

E Lifeline

Our modern, fully-equipped gym is open to members seven days a week with 25 different classes, each suitable for a range of fitness levels. Whether you want to lose weight or recover from an injury, we can offer you a professional personal trainer to help you achieve your goals.

6.1) The wind was blowing hard

Language practice

1 Find ten travel words in the word square.

E	B	O	A	R	D	I	N	A	N
P	T	L	Y	F	A	N	D	N	O
L	I	U	F	A	S	T	E	N	L
A	M	P	Z	F	E	E	K	O	E
T	E	M	I	S	S	A	N	U	Q
F	T	R	Q	C	A	B	I	N	U
O	A	K	U	D	L	L	M	C	S
R	B	P	I	P	L	A	N	E	X
M	L	I	N	Y	H	W	A	M	Y
H	E	L	I	C	O	P	T	E	R
C	X	O	T	H	R	E	L	N	G
A	T	T	Y	J	U	S	P	T	A

2 Use the words in Activity 1 to complete these sentences about travel.

1 They give you a card at the airport check-in desk which you must show before you can _board_ the _____.
2 We'd just found our seats in the _____ when the flight attendant told us to _____ our seat belts ready for take-off.
3 Tom is training to be an air ambulance _____ . He's delighted because he's always wanted to fly a _____.
4 The station was full of people waiting on the _____ when there was an _____ that the train was cancelled.
5 I think we should hurry, I don't want to _____ the bus - according to the _____ it leaves in five minutes.

3 Read the email and choose the correct tense, past simple or past continuous.

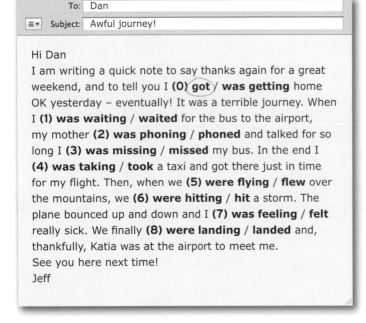

To: Dan

Subject: Awful journey!

Hi Dan
I am writing a quick note to say thanks again for a great weekend, and to tell you I **(0) got / was getting** home OK yesterday – eventually! It was a terrible journey. When I **(1) was waiting / waited** for the bus to the airport, my mother **(2) was phoning / phoned** and talked for so long I **(3) was missing / missed** my bus. In the end I **(4) was taking / took** a taxi and got there just in time for my flight. Then, when we **(5) were flying / flew** over the mountains, we **(6) were hitting / hit** a storm. The plane bounced up and down and I **(7) was feeling / felt** really sick. We finally **(8) were landing / landed** and, thankfully, Katia was at the airport to meet me.
See you here next time!
Jeff

Exam practice: Writing part 3

4 Answer this exam question.

• This is part of a letter you receive from an English friend.
• Now write a letter to your friend, answering the questions.
• Write your letter in about 100 words.

I've just got back from Australia - it was a 27-hour flight! Tell me about the longest journey you've ever made. Where did you go and how did you travel? What was the journey like?

6.2 Into the rainforest

Language practice

1 Try this quiz to see how much you know about the rainforest. Choose A, B or C.

0 Around a quarter of the world's rainforests are in ___Brazil___ .
(A Brazil)   B Russia   C Nepal

1 A quarter of the ingredients in our _____ come from rainforest plants.
A make-up   B medicine   C food

2 Twenty-five acres of rainforest in Borneo has more than 700 species
of _____ – more than the whole of the USA.
A tree   B monkey   C leaf

3 One in five of all the _____ in the world live in the rainforests of the Amazon.
A lakes   B birds   C crocodiles

4 20 percent of the world's _____ is found in the Amazon.
A rain water   B sea water   C fresh water

2 Join these sentences using the words in brackets.

0 Our walk in the forest was brilliant. We were bitten by insects.   (even though)
Our walk in the forest was brilliant, even though we were bitten by insects.
1 Everyone enjoyed themselves. The weather was wet.   (despite)
2 We saw some beautiful parrots. We didn't find any monkeys.   (Although)
3 We managed to climb to the top of the cliff. Our bags were heavy.   (in spite of)
4 I don't like snakes. I'm glad they're protected.   (although)
5 We swam in the lake. The water was freezing.   (in spite of)

Exam practice: Reading Part 5

3 Read the text below and choose the correct word for each space. For each question, circle the correct letter A, B, C or D.

RAINFOREST ANIMALS

Scientists believe that rainforests **(0)** ___may___ be home to more than ten million different forms of wildlife. The largest group **(1)** _____ of insects, which climb or fly easily from tree to tree. Most people are familiar **(2)** _____ colourful parrots, but they are only one part of the total bird **(3)** _____ , which goes from tiny hummingbirds to huge toucans. Many rainforest animals have developed for living in the treetops. Some monkeys have thin webs of skin between their legs that **(4)** _____ them to almost fly between **(5)** _____ . Others have long, strong tails, like an **(6)** _____ arm, so they can hang down to **(7)** _____ pieces of fruit.

(8) _____ the weather is so hot and damp during the day, most forest creatures are active during the **(9)** _____ of darkness. And a large number of animals, including great apes, big cats and **(10)** _____ elephants, live on the forest floor.

0	A may	B can	C should	D would
1	A keeps	B consists	C holds	D claims
2	A with	B to	C of	D by
3	A set	B company	C population	D society
4	A let	B allow	C make	D admit
5	A branches	B leaves	C flowers	D plants
6	A accurate	B equal	C extra	D alive
7	A contact	B achieve	C approach	D reach
8	A Although	B When	C Since	D Unless
9	A hours	B days	C seasons	D times
10	A only	B almost	C hardly	D even

Winners and losers

7.1 I could easily swim further

Language practice

1 Use the clues to complete the puzzle. What is the highlighted word?

1 You need this for surfing on the sea or snow.
2 You kick the ball into the net to score this.
3 Hockey and football are played on this.
4 You run races on this.
5 This protects your head.
6 This is a word for running and jumping, etc.

2 Complete the sentences with a comparative or superlative adverb formed from one of the adjectives in the box.

bad   careful   easy   frequent   good

0 My sister drives _more carefully_ than Lewis Hamilton.
1 You will be able to run faster if you train _____ than you do now.
2 Torres was 'man of the match' because he played _____.
3 You can ride a bike _____ when the wind is behind you.
4 I came last because I swam _____!

Exam practice: Reading Part 3

3 Look at the sentences below about adventure racing. Read the text to decide if each sentence is correct or incorrect. If it is correct, put a tick (✔) in the box under A for YES. If it is not correct, put a tick (✔) in the box under B for NO.

	A: YES	B: NO
1 Adventure racing takes place at traditional sporting venues.	☐	☐
2 An event for first-time racers usually includes three different sporting skills.	☐	☐
3 Adventure racers sometimes have to climb the walls of tall buildings.	☐	☐
4 The tests for racers at checkpoints are designed to measure their levels of fitness.	☐	☐
5 There is an age limit for competitors.	☐	☐
6 There are organised opportunities for racers to improve their racing skills.	☐	☐

Adventure racing

Adventure racing developed from the triathlon, the three-part athletics event in which athletes race on foot, on bikes and in the water. During the 1980s athletes added a range of other activities, and adventure racing was born.

A typical adventure race for beginners lasts 4–6 hours and includes swimming in a lake or river, mountain biking and running across rough countryside. Advanced-level races can be over several days and may include sports such as rock-climbing, mountaineering, roller-skating or skiing. A city event might include biking down stone stairs, getting through a large pipe or descending on a rope from the top of a block of flats.

Adventure races include checkpoints along the route, where racers are given tasks designed to test their ability to think clearly when physically very tired. For this reason, adventure racing is known as a 'thought sport': winning or losing depends not only on speed and strength, but also on skills such as map-reading, planning and decision-making.

Almost anyone can try adventure racing, but for insurance purposes, you have to be 18 or over. For entry-level races you should be able to swim 1 kilometre, cycle 20 kilometres and run 5 kilometres. However, the ability to keep going without giving up is just as important as your sporting skill.

If you decide to take adventure racing further, there are weekend training camps where you can learn more about various aspects of the sport, for example bike-handling, climbing down a cliff or race preparation! These courses usually end with a race in which you can try out what you have just learned.

He has just won first prize

Language practice

1 Complete the text with these words.

| ago | already | at first | for | now | since | yet |

Eight years **(0)** _ago_ Amanda Strong started entering competitions in magazines and newspapers.
(1) _____ then she has won hundreds of prizes and hasn't paid for a holiday **(2)** _____ a long time. **(3)** _____ her family thought Amanda's hobby was a joke, but **(4)** _____ they've changed their minds! Amanda has **(5)** _____ taken her sister on a cruise to the Caribbean this year. The rest of her family haven't booked a holiday **(6)** _____ . They're waiting to see what Amanda wins!

Exam practice: Reading Part 4

2 Read the text and questions below. For each question, circle the correct letter, A, B, C or D.

My name's John Martin. Last summer, I went to London to meet Lorna Black, the head of an organisation that makes sure the voices of young people are heard. As a school student, I was invited to join the judges for a competition called 'Yell!'. The people who entered had to create an artwork – a picture, a film or a photo – showing one of the problems that young people face in society today.

Although Lorna and her colleagues had managed to select 30 finalists from the 3,000 entries, it was still really difficult to choose the winners. Of course I wanted the best entry to succeed, but I also didn't want to disappoint anyone. Judging the younger age group was particularly hard because, having a younger sister, I know how upset kids can get if they don't win.

The panel of four judges consisted of myself, Ali Lewis, lead singer of the band Popart, Helen Rivera, art designer of a daily newspaper, and Victor Staton, editor of a magazine for young people. I didn't always agree with their opinions, but it was a great challenge to work beside them as an equal, and an experience I will never forget.

1 What is the writer doing in the text?
   A inviting young people to judge a competition
   B encouraging school students to enter a competition
   C explaining how the winners of a competition were chosen
   D describing his role in a competition

2 Lorna Black works for an organisation that
   A makes films about young people.
   B makes sure young people are listened to.
   C deals with young people's problems.
   D organises societies for young people.

3 The writer found his job difficult because
   A he felt sorry for the losers.
   B all the entries were so good.
   C there were too many finalists.
   D he wanted his sister to win.

4 What would the writer say about the judges?
   A There weren't any disagreements, despite the difference in our ages.
   B I felt that they looked down on me and didn't understand me.
   C They respected my opinions even though I was the youngest.
   D They were all experts so I wasn't able to say what I really thought.

8.1 Students don't have to study!

Language practice

1 Read the rules below and complete the email using *don't have to*, *can't*, *have to* or *can*.

Hilldown English Summer School - School Rules

1 Rooms must be kept tidy. All students must make their own beds.
2 Do not move the furniture in your room.
3 Laundry will be collected once a week.
4 Students must be on time for classes and meals.
5 Students who miss a morning class because of illness are not allowed to go out in the evening.
6 Organised trips and activities are available, but taking part is up to you.
7 The library is open all day and you have free access to the internet.

☰▼ **Subject:** Hello from Hilldown!

Dear Margarita,
I'm enjoying my English course but there are lots of rules! We **(0)** *have to* keep our rooms tidy and we **(1)** _____ move the furniture around. We **(2)** _____ do our own laundry, luckily! We **(3)** _____ be on time for all meals and classes and if we miss a class, then we **(4)** _____ go out in the evening. There are organised trips, but we **(5)** _____ go on those if we don't want to! We **(6)** _____ go to the library whenever we want and we **(7)** _____ pay to use the computers, so I **(8)** _____ check my emails whenever I want to!
Take care,
Josephine

---

2 Imagine that Josephine has finished her course. Rewrite her email in the past tense.

I enjoyed my English course, but there were lots of rules! We had to ...

Exam practice: Reading Part 2

3 These people all want to do an art course. Below are descriptions of five courses. Decide which course would be the most suitable for the following people.

1 Akio is an experienced artist looking for an enjoyable course where he can improve his skills. He enjoys painting outdoors and is free in the afternoons.

2 Jo is free during the day. She doesn't paint, but loves modern art and would like to learn more about it. She hopes to avoid spending all her time in the classroom.

3 Hugo draws in his free time, but would like to be able to earn money from it as he is bored with his current job. He can attend classes in the evening or at the weekend.

A Complete beginners will learn how to create art based on their everyday experience. The course will explore subjects such as the street, the city, and friends and family. Students will also research a modern artist of their choice in order to become familiar with the language of painting. Classes are on Fridays, 2.30-4.30 p.m.

B This course is for anyone looking for a new hobby or a career change. Students will study some drawing techniques and will also be introduced to the main areas of the cartoon industry, including drawing for books and newspapers. There is also advice on how to sell your work. Classes are on Mondays, 6.30-9.00 p.m.

C This is a fun course, taught by a professional artist. Most lessons will take place in the countryside, where students will learn new techniques, not only from the teacher, but also from one another. The course takes place on Tuesdays, 1.30-5.00 p.m.

D This course aims to provide an enjoyable introduction to the most important art from the Renaissance to the late 19th century. The course will focus on looking works of art and discussing them, and will help students decide whether to study the subject further. The course takes place on Tuesdays, 10.30 a.m.-12.00 p.m.

E This course looks at some of the most important art in the 20th and 21st century. Students will learn about a wide variety of artists, and will discuss the ideas behind their work. The course will include lectures, discussions and films, along with museum and gallery visits. Classes take place on Thursdays from 1.00-3.00 p.m.

8.2 A job that you enjoy

Language practice

1 Join these sentences with a relative pronoun to make one sentence.

0 There's the internet café. I left my bag there.
There's the internet café where I left my bag.
1 That's the woman. Her son is a pop star.
2 I live in the village. I was born there.
3 I moved here in 2006. In 2006 I got this job.
4 I saw a film last night. It starred Johnny Depp.

2 Add *-er*, *-ist* or *-or* to make jobs from these words. You may need to make other changes.

0 instruct *instructor*	3 report _____	6 manage _____	9 interpret _____
1 novel _____	4 art _____	7 design _____	10 guitar _____
2 photograph _____	5 science _____	8 sail _____	11 football _____

Exam practice: Reading Part 5

3 Read the text below and choose the correct word for each space. For each question, circle the correct letter A, B, C or D.

Interview Technique

Most people find the thought **(0)** ___of___ a job interview terrifying. However, it is important not to be too **(1)** _____ on the day, because this could **(2)** _____ your chances of getting the job. The best **(3)** _____ to beat the fear is to be very well **(4)** _____ . Research everything you can about the company and the person who will be interviewing you. This will help you feel more in **(5)** _____ of the situation, and you will impress the interviewer with your knowledge.

Find out your best route to the interview and make sure you know how **(6)** _____ it will take you to get there. Decide **(7)** _____ you are going to wear the night before the interview. Choose something you feel comfortable in, **(8)** _____ which makes you look smart and successful. And finally, on arriving at the reception desk, **(9)** _____ polite to the staff there. You never know whose opinion matters most in a company – after all, the receptionist **(10)** _____ be married to the person who is interviewing you!

	A	B	C	D
0	(A of)	B for	C by	D to
1	A stressful	B terrible	C angry	D nervous
2	A stop	B spoil	C hold	D break
3	A means	B manner	C way	D system
4	A prepared	B produced	C placed	D planned
5	A power	B control	C rule	D influence
6	A late	B far	C time	D long
7	A what	B that	C why	D when
8	A but	B despite	C except	D although
9	A get	B stay	C be	D have
10	A must	B might	C should	D would

Exam practice: Writing Part 3

4 Answer this exam question.

- This is part of a letter you receive from your English friend, Stefan.
- Now write a letter to Stefan telling him about your school.
- Write your letter in about 100 words.

> I've just started at a new school. I like it, but it's very different from my old school. What's your school like? What kind of rules are there? Write soon and tell me all about it.

9.1 We will have robots

Language practice

1 Put the words in the correct order to make sentences about life in 50 years' time.

0 will / us / Robots / everyday / in / our / help / lives /.
Robots will help us in our everyday lives.

1 years / probably / People / live / several / for / will / hundred /.

2 be / cash / unlikely / for / is / any / There / need / to /.

3 download / a / We / be / may / to / memories / our / onto / computer / able /.

4 might / pets / future / robots / the / of / the / be / 'Intelligent' /.

5 around / driverless / travel / will / cars / We / in /.

2 Which sentences in Activity 1 do you think will definitely happen? Which do you think might happen?

Exam practice: Reading Part 4

3 Read the text about an underwater camera and the questions below. For each question circle the correct letter, A, B, C or D.

Digital underwater camera mask

Hardly anyone uses a film camera any more, but I often bought the single-use, underwater kind for holidays. However, even that may soon disappear with the appearance of this unusual type of camera in the shops. To see how good it is, I spent an afternoon under water with a couple of friends, in my neighbour's pool.

The camera was easy to use, but felt a little heavier than a normal swimming mask. There are large, colourful buttons for taking the pictures and starting or stopping the video. The camera cleverly turns off after two minutes if you don't use it, which should help save batteries. It comes with some rather unnecessary software which never reached my CD-drive.

The camera works to a depth of about five metres, and this is plenty for most swimmers. There's no flash, which could be a problem for cloudy days in a dark ocean, but didn't matter to us in the swimming pool. Also, it needs about a second between photos, so you might miss some of those fast-moving fish. However, my toughest challenge was learning how to aim. In the beginning I kept taking photos of people's feet instead of their faces! All in all though, this is a great camera and one I'd happily recommend.

1 What is the writer doing in this text?
  A writing a review of a new product
  B suggesting improvements to a product
  C explaining the advantages of digital cameras
  D describing photos he took on holiday

2 What did the writer especially like about the camera?
  A the software that came with it
  B the fact that it isn't too heavy
  C the way the large, colourful buttons were designed
  D the fact that it stops working when not in use

3 Which of the following would the writer say about the camera?

A It made me quite angry that I had to wait so long between pictures.

C The most difficult thing was getting exactly the picture I wanted.

B It was a real shame that I couldn't use the camera in dark conditions.

D I was very disappointed that I couldn't take the camera deeper than five metres.

9.2 Unless we act now ...

Language practice

1 Make questions and affirmative and negative sentences with *going to*.

0 snow / tomorrow / ?
  Is it going to snow tomorrow?
1 I / write to some politicians about global warming / ✔
2 you / recycle that bottle / ?
3 rain / this afternoon / ✗
4 Some parts of the world / have more droughts in the future / ✔

5 I / leave the TV on standby any more / ✗
6 Mr Jones / ask us to write a report about our visit to the exhibition / ?
7 There / be a storm tonight / ✔
8 We / switch on the central heating / ✗
9 Tigers / become extinct / ?
10 I / help clean up the beach on Saturday / ✔

2 Put the verbs in brackets into the correct tense, present simple or *will*.

0 I ___won't go___ (not go) to the beach tomorrow unless it ___is___ (be) really hot and sunny.
1 If it _____ (not stop) raining soon, there _____ (be) a flood.
2 We _____ (not be able) to go to school unless it _____ (stop) snowing.
3 If we _____ (not protect) the rainforests, many animals _____ (become) extinct.
4 I _____ (meet) you outside the exhibition at 9.00 a.m., unless I _____ (be) late!
5 Mr Kos _____ (not mark) our projects unless we _____ (give) them to him on time.
6 I _____ (drive) more carefully tonight if the roads _____ (be) icy.
7 If you _____ (count) the seconds between lightning and thunder, you _____ (can tell) how far away a storm is.
8 Unless it _____ (rain) soon, most of these plants _____ (die).

Exam practice: Writing Part 3

3 Answer this exam question.

• Your English teacher has asked you to write a story.
• Your story must have the following title:
  The big storm
• Write your story in about 100 words.

Exam practice: Writing Part 1

4 Here are some sentences about how one school is helping the environment. For each question, complete the second sentence so that it means the same as the first. Use no more than three words.

0 At our school we try our hardest to help the environment.
  At our school we do our ___best___ to help the environment
1 Many children walk to school instead of coming by car.
  Many children come to school on _____ instead of coming by car.
2 Kitchen staff throw away less food than they used to.
  Kitchen staff don't throw away _____ food as they used to.
3 Children bring drinks in re-usable bottles.
  Children bring drinks in bottles that they can _____ again.
4 In the playground, there are special bins for drinks cans.
  The playground _____ special bins for drinks cans.
5 We can help to protect the environment if we all work together.
  We can't help to protect the environment _____ we all work together.

10.1 If I visited your country ...

Language practice

1 Match the ideas. What might the boy in the picture say? There may be more than one possible answer.

0 stay in a hotel
1 stay at the seaside
2 be more kids on this campsite
3 campsite have a pool
4 Mum and Dad let me bring a friend
5 be a town nearby
6 weather be better

A have fun on the beach
B go out together in the evening
C find some shops selling computer games.
D not feel so miserable
E go for a swim
F sleep in a proper bed
G organise a game of football

2 Make second conditional sentences using the ideas from Activity 1.

0 *If we stayed in a hotel, I could sleep in a proper bed.*

Exam practice: Reading Part 1

3 Look at the text in each question. What does it say? Circle the correct letter A, B or C.

1 *Mark*
I've arranged flights. No tickets, we just show our booking number and passports at the check-in desk. Can you check bus times to the airport?
Rob

Rob wants Mark to

A meet him at the check-in desk.
B find out about transport to the airport.
C let him know his passport number.

2 *Josh*
What do you think about going to Adventure World on Friday? We have to sign the list before Tuesday if we're interested. If you go, I'll go too.
Katie

Why has Katie emailed Josh about Adventure World?

A She doesn't want to go on the trip alone.
B She wants Josh to take her there on Tuesday.
C She doesn't have enough information about it.

3
Chelsworth Zoo
One free teacher ticket
for every five student tickets bought

A Groups of five students must have a teacher with them.
B To get in for nothing, a teacher must buy five student tickets.
C Teachers can get six student tickets for the price of five.

4 *I enjoyed seeing the city from the river on this sightseeing cruise, but we couldn't get off anywhere so I'm looking forward to visiting the sights on foot tomorrow.*
Meg

A Meg was disappointed with the river trip.
B Meg has already been to most of the city sights.
C Meg is planning to walk around part of the city.

10.2 CDs can be bought online

Language practice

1 Add these words to the sets below.

> audience   discount   guitar   tent   tickets

1 sold out   online   book   _tickets_   _____
2 campsite   put up   sleeping bag   _____

3 electric   play   rock   _____
4 clap   seats   interval   _____

2 Complete the notice with these words.

> brought   collected   recorded   ~~switched~~   taken

Philharmonia Hall

- Mobiles should be **(0)** _switched_ to silent during the performance.
- No food or drink may be **(1)** _____ into the concert hall.
- No part of this concert may be **(2)** _____.
- Photographs must not be **(3)** _____ inside the concert hall.
- Tickets booked by phone can be **(4)** _____ from the box office.

3 Look at the information from a music festival website. Complete the second sentence in each question so that it means the same as the first.

0 Children of 12 and under must be accompanied by an adult.
 Children of 12 and under _must have_ an adult with them.
1 As the weather can change quickly, both rainwear and suncream should be packed.
 You _____ both rainwear and suncream as the weather can change quickly.
2 A festival map and programme can be collected at the entrance on arrival.
 You _____ a festival map and programme at the entrance when you arrive.
3 Don't bring too much as all camping equipment must be carried from the car park to the campsite.
 Don't bring too much as you _____ all camping equipment from the car park to the campsite.
4 Mobiles may be used, but should be kept in a safe place.
 You _____ your mobile but you _____ it in a safe place.
5 Water bottles can be filled for free from the taps around the site.
 You _____ your water bottles for free from the taps around the site.
6 Tents must not be set up before the festival officially opens at 8 a.m. on Wednesday.
 You _____ your tent before the festival officially opens at 8 a.m. on Wednesday.

Exam practice: Writing Part 2

4 You and your English friend, Charlie, are going to spend next Saturday at a music festival. Write an email to Charlie.

In your email, you should

- suggest a suitable time to meet Charlie
- explain how you will both get to the festival
- remind Charlie of what to bring.

Write 35–45 words.

Language practice

1 Complete the sentences with these words.

like   same   like   same   like   similar   same

0 When I got to the party I saw that a girl was wearing a dress just ____*like*____ mine.
1 Your computer game is _____ to mine but it's not exactly the _____ .
2 He bought his boots and his jacket in the _____ shop.
3 I'm looking for a bag _____ the one I saw in this magazine.
4 I'm not a shopoholic _____ you – I hate shopping!
5 Your new shoes are the _____ as your old ones! Why didn't you buy something a bit different?

2 Match the clothes to the occasions. Then put the words in the correct order in a sentence.

0 a / grey / smart / dark / suit
1 a pair of / leather / strong / waterproof / boots
2 a / floor-length / silk / beautiful / dress
3 a pair of / soft / cotton / comfortable / pyjamas
4 a / bright / stripy / new / blue / swimming costume

A going on holiday
B going to bed
C going to work
D going to a party
E going for a long walk

0 *My brother wears a smart dark grey suit to go to work.*

Exam practice: Reading Part 5

3 Read the text below and choose the correct word for each space. For each question, circle the correct letter, A, B, C or D.

Agyness Deyn

The model Agyness Deyn was born Laura Hollins **(0)** _____on_____ 16 February 1983. Many people **(1)** _____ her to be the next great supermodel of the fashion **(2)** _____. The unusual **(3)** _____ of her hair and brightly-coloured clothes make her stand out from the crowd. Unlike many **(4)** _____ models, Agyness doesn't only appear in public **(5)** _____ the latest fashions. She likes to **(6)** _____ fun with her clothes, and the way she dresses **(7)** _____ that she is a lively and creative person.

At the age of fourteen, she began working in a fish and chip shop in Manchester. Two years later, she moved to London, where she worked in a burger bar **(8)** _____ the daytime and at a night club in the evenings. When she was eighteen, she **(9)** _____ with a model agency called Models 1. Her best friend is the designer Henry Holland, **(10)** _____ used to be a customer of hers at the fish and chip shop. She is now the 'face' of his company.

	A	B	C	D
0	on	by	in	at
1	say	consider	see	suggest
2	company	firm	industry	organisation
3	shape	design	form	style
4	other	extra	further	additional
5	showing	wearing	using	having
6	have	make	do	take
7	tells	shows	says	displays
8	since	until	during	for
9	joined	connected	registered	attended
10	which	whose	what	who

11.2 I've had my hair cut

Language practice

1 Look at the pictures. Write what the people need to have / get done.

 **0**  **1**  **2**  **3**  **4**

| car / repair | house / paint | hair / cut | eyes / test | dress / clean |

0 He *needs to have/get his car repaired* .

1 She _____ .

2 He _____ .

3 He _____ .

4 She _____ .

Exam practice: Reading Part 3

2 Look at the sentences below about Bloomingdale's, a department store in New York.
Read the text to decide if each sentence is correct or incorrect. If it is correct, put a tick (✔) in the box under A for YES. If it is not correct, put a tick (✔) in the box under B for NO.

A: YES   B: NO

1 The brothers Lyman and Joseph called their first shop 'Bloomingdale's'. ☐ ☐
2 Lyman and Joseph sold a range of different clothes in their shop. ☐ ☐
3 The brothers moved their shop because business was bad on the old site. ☐ ☐
4 From its earliest days, Bloomingdale's attracted customers with a lot of money. ☐ ☐
5 People had to visit Bloomingdale's to find out what they sold. ☐ ☐
6 Lyman organised special events for the public at Bloomingdale's. ☐ ☐
7 Bloomingdale's designer shopping bags can be worth a lot of money. ☐ ☐
8 The store began to attract younger customers in the 1970s. ☐ ☐
9 Bloomingdale stores can be found in many countries around the world. ☐ ☐

Bloomingdale's
store history

When the Bloomingdale brothers started doing business in New York City in 1872, clothes shops usually sold just one thing. But brothers Lyman and Joseph's new shop, known as the Great East Side Bazaar, carried a variety of items such as gloves, hats, skirts and underwear. It was the beginning of what would become a 'department store'.

The shop was very successful and, in 1886, the brothers relocated to 59th Street and Lexington Avenue. This area of town was home to many wealthy people and, of course, to their servants. It was to this group of workers – not their employers – that Bloomingdale's originally aimed its services.

Bloomingdale's was always looking for new ways to bring in customers. Lyman advertised in newspapers and on posters to let people know about the store's products and prices. He had some interesting ideas of how to make Bloomingdale's more popular. For example, he was one of the first to install elevators, or 'sky carriages' as he called them. The store also became the venue for fashion shows and other important occasions, including 'Woman of the Year 1947'.

In the 1960s, Bloomingdale's team came up with the first designer shopping bags. Since then many of these have become collectors' items and people pay a great deal for them. By the 1970s, the store was famous around the world. Even Queen Elizabeth paid a visit. For the first time in its history, it became fashionable with the under-25s. These days there are 36 Bloomingdale's stores in the USA and there are plans to open more. The first Bloomingdale's outside the USA is due to open in 2010 in Dubai.

12.1 I'd never seen a film before

Language practice

1 Complete the sentences using simple past or past perfect.

0 Last weekend my friends and I ___decided___ (decide) to go to the cinema.

1 We _____ (look) on the internet and _____ (choose) a film that none of us _____ (see).

2 John _____ (pass) his driving test the week before so he _____ (offer) to drive us.

3 Unfortunately none of us _____ (go) to that cinema before and we _____ (get) terribly lost.

4 By the time we _____ (get) to the cinema, the film _____ (start).

Exam practice: Reading Part 2

2 The people below all want to see a film. Read the descriptions of five films. Decide which film would be most suitable for the following people.

1  Antonio enjoys watching films with complicated stories that demand his attention. He likes films with plenty of action, as he gets bored quite easily.

2  Julia has two children aged 10 and 12, who love comedies. Julia prefers drama, but would like to find a film that they will all enjoy.

3  Jozef likes exciting films set in beautiful landscapes. He particularly enjoys films about real people who follow their dream despite facing many difficulties on the way.

A Famous at Last
Toby and Amelia win a competition to star in a TV documentary about their lives. What they don't realise is that the show will become a huge success and that their lives will never be the same again. Younger audiences will find plenty to laugh at in this movie, but it does have a serious message as well about the price of fame.

B Escape
This entertaining film is based on a true story. A teenage criminal steals millions of dollars and then goes on the run. The film explores the developing relationship between him and the detective who is chasing him. This is quite a serious film, so don't expect car chases and gun fights – you'll be disappointed.

C Remember
The last thing Anna remembers is the murder of her son. Despite having no memory from that day on, she is determined to find his killer. This exciting, eventful film is split into two separate stories, one going back in time and one going forward. You have to concentrate throughout or you will get completely lost, but it's worth the effort!

D Flying Phoebe
This film tells the true story of Australian, Tim Starr, whose life-long ambition was to take his 1930s motorcycle, which he called 'Phoebe', to the Atacama desert in Chile, to test its speed. Tim battles with ill-health and lack of money. He eventually makes it to Chile, but will the motorbike perform as he hopes? There is never a dull moment in this story.

E Clowns Allowed
Adrian dreams of becoming a clown and runs away from home to join the circus. He is helped by ex-clown Mikey, who agrees to teach him everything he knows. Children will certainly find this comedy very amusing, but there is little depth to the story and the adults sitting with them may wish they were elsewhere.

12.2 My agent asked me to work

Language practice

1 Read the conversation and report what the people say.

0	Journalist:	What happened?
1	Sam:	I saw a strange light in the sky.
2	Journalist:	Can you describe the light?
3	Sam:	It was long and blue, and it moved very fast.
4	Journalist:	Where was the light?
5	Sam:	I saw it over the clock tower and then it disappeared in the direction of the castle.
6	Journalist:	Oh no! It sounds like the Saturn Soldiers are back!

0 *The journalist asked Sam what had happened.*

2 What is the speaker doing in each sentence? Choose the correct word to complete the second sentence.

0 James said, 'I'll do my homework as soon as this programme finishes.'
James (**persuaded** / **promised**) to do his homework as soon as the programme finished.

1 The waitress said to me, 'Don't touch that plate, it's very hot.'
The waitress (**warned** / **complained**) me not to touch the plate because it was very hot.

2 My brother said, 'Why don't we go shopping to get Mum a present?'
My brother (**reminded** / **suggested**) that we go shopping to get Mum a present.

3 'Don't touch my MP3 player!' I said to my sister.
I (**explained** / **told**) my sister not to touch my MP3 player.

4 'The producer of a film is the person who provides the money,' my dad said.
My father (**offered** / **explained**) that the producer of a film is the person who provides the money.

5 'I'm sorry I'm late,' the teacher said to the class.
The teacher (**apologised** / **persuaded**) to the class for being late.

Exam practice: Writing Part 1

3 Here are some sentences about someone's career in the film industry. For each question, complete the second sentence so that it means the same as the first. Use no more than three words.

0 Matt started working in the film industry when he was 18.
Matt __*has worked*__ in the film industry since he was 18.

1 Matt directed his first film when he was 22 years old.
Matt directed his first film at _____ of 22.

2 Matt wasn't given much time to make the film by the producers.
The producers _____ Matt much time to make the film.

3 Matt said that lots of things had gone wrong during filming.
Matt said, 'Lots of things _____ wrong during filming.'

4 Making the film was much harder than Matt had expected.
Making the film wasn't as _____ Matt had expected.

5 The film got good reviews, but it didn't make much money.
The film got good reviews even _____ it didn't make much money.

Reading and Writing Paper

Reading

Part 1

Questions 1–5

Look at the text in each question.
What does it say?
Mark the correct letter **A**, **B**, or **C** on your answer sheet.

Example:

0

> Only **two** places left in Mr Jones's guitar club – book now to avoid disappointment.

A   You need to hurry if you want to join the guitar club.

B   The guitar club is now full until next term.

C   Unless two more people join, the guitar club will close.

Answer:

0	A ■	B ☐	C ☐

1

> *Goldenfields Holiday Homes*
>
> A minimum of three days' notice is required to change your departure date

A   It is unlikely that we will be able to change your departure date.

B   Tell us of any change to your departure date at least three days in advance.

C   We'll change your departure date if you stay for at least three extra days.

2

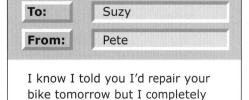

To:	Suzy
From:	Pete

I know I told you I'd repair your bike tomorrow but I completely forgot about a family party I have to go to – really sorry!

Why is Pete apologising to Suzy?

A   He can't go to the party with her.

B   He can't do the favour he had promised.

C   He hasn't had time to repair her bike.

3

Anyone wanting to play basketball for the school should go to the gym at 4 p.m. on Thursday. If selected, you must be available on Tuesday afternoons for team practice.

A   The school is looking for new people to join the basketball team.

B   The time of the basketball team's practice session has been changed.

C   There will be an extra practice this week for members of the basketball team.

4

✆ message

Jason – your piano teacher rang. You left your music book at his house after the lesson. He says he can bring it round any time today or tomorrow.
Mum

Jason needs to

A   collect his book from the piano teacher's house.

B   ask someone to lend him a book for tomorrow's lesson.

C   let the piano teacher know when to return the book.

5

☆ **BOX OFFICE** ☆

....

Check tickets carefully – we are not responsible for mistakes discovered later

A   Make sure everything is correct before you leave.

B   We will correct any mistakes we have made with your ticket.

C   We will only correct mistakes that our staff are responsible for.

Part 2

Questions 6–10

The people on this page all want to go on an adventure holiday.
On the opposite page there are descriptions of eight holidays.
Decide which holiday would be the most suitable for the following people.
For questions 6–10, mark the correct letter (A–H) on your answer sheet.

_____

6  Tony is going on holiday by himself, but hopes to meet other people. He enjoys walking and seeing wildlife but wants to start in a city, to learn more about the country's customs.

7  Nishiko and Alice want to go on a trip where they can get involved in a project to help local people. They also want to explore the area and have time to relax.

8  Simon and Jasmine like quiet, relaxing holidays but their teenage children prefer to be more active. They are looking for a holiday that will suit them all.

9  Alex has never tried a watersport and would like to do so on this holiday. He enjoys going out in the evening and would like to stay somewhere simple and inexpensive.

10  Samantha is studying to become an architect and enjoys holidays where she can follow this interest. She would also like to try some exciting outdoor activities.

Adventure Holidays

A   Turkey

The small fishing town of Kas is a great place for action and adventure in the outdoors, and this holiday really proves it. Designed with teenagers in mind, there is never a dull moment. The package includes trips sailing, diving, snorkelling and rock climbing.

B   Slovakia

Join an important Slovakian wildlife project. Working with expert guides, you will search for bears, wolves and wildcats. Accommodation is in simple mountain cottages. The work that you do here will help keep the populations of animals healthy.

C   Nepal

After exploring the traditions and culture of the capital, Kathmandu, we'll travel into the Himalayas, going on foot into some remote villages. The trip finishes in Chitwan National Park, where we will explore the jungle by elephant. This holiday is suitable for either groups or individuals travelling on their own, and many friendships have been made on our holidays.

D   Dominican Republic

If you've never tried surfing before and want to have some lessons, then this is the perfect place to do it. Accommodation is very basic, but that helps keep the cost down. As well as surfing, there's the jungle nearby and the nightlife is very lively.

E   France

Your holiday begins with a canoe trip down the Ardèche river, to see the local wildlife and amazing views of the valley. Later in the week we'll explore the area on horseback and try some rock climbing. We'll also visit the medieval city of Avignon to look at the city's magnificent buildings and bridges.

F   Thailand

After spending time in one of the region's oldest rainforests, you'll receive a warm welcome as the guests of a rural village. Your work here could involve teaching in the local school, building a health centre or helping the elderly collect water. The nearby beaches are beautiful, and perfect for quiet restful days.

G   The Canary Islands

The aim of this holiday is to provide a safe and enjoyable introduction to the sport of kite boarding. Accommodation is in a brand new luxury apartment block a short walk from the beach. This trip is great for those travelling alone or with friends.

H   Egypt

This trip to the Red Sea allows you to create your own perfect holiday. You can choose how you spend your days – join one of our groups riding a camel in the desert, go diving (if you have a qualification), rent a bike, or simply find a quiet spot on the beach to read your book.

Part 3

Questions 11–20

Look at the sentences below about working at a school in India.
Read the text on the opposite page to decide if each sentence is correct or incorrect.
If it is correct, mark **A** on your answer sheet.
If it is not correct, mark **B** on your answer sheet.

---

11 Elise applied directly to the school for the teaching post.

12 The course in Delhi prepared members for their work and for everyday life.

13 This was Elise's first experience of working in a school.

14 The children's home was situated high in the mountains.

15 The majority of the pupils in the school lived in the children's home.

16 Elise and Lucy were upset that the children were so curious about them.

17 It was a challenge to interest all the pupils in the general knowledge lessons.

18 Elise and Lucy wanted to punish the children if they were bad in class.

19 Sports lessons were a recent addition to the school's curriculum.

20 When Elise played football with the boys she scored a goal for her team.

Teaching in India

by Elise Cooper

'Elise in India'. That was the name of my blog last year when I took a year out between school and university. I was lucky enough to get a teaching job abroad through an international organisation. I was going to work in a school attached to a children's home in north-west India. There were eight of us on the week-long introduction course in the capital, Delhi. As well as advice and ideas for teaching we were given information about health and local customs, and learned a few essential phrases in the local language.

Another course member, Lucy, was coming to the same school as me and we were both nervous when we set off on the 15-hour bus ride to the children's home. I had worked as a classroom assistant before, but here I wouldn't be much older than some of my pupils. How would I manage? My worries disappeared once we reached the home. Our rooms were on the top floor above the girls' bedrooms and from the window we looked out across flat fields full of fruit trees and could just see the snow-covered mountain tops in the distance.

There were 90 children in the home, aged between five and 20. In addition there were a small number of pupils who came in each day from the area around. Although they were a little shy to start with, they were so keen to ask us questions that we quickly became friends.

Lucy and I taught four lessons a day, mainly spelling, reading and general knowledge. We had a textbook but since it wasn't very exciting, we tried to make the lessons more interesting with activities and games. This wasn't always easy: there was a mixture of ages in each class because pupils had begun their education at different times. Like schoolchildren everywhere, they didn't always behave perfectly in class. However, they used to send us notes apologising afterwards, or thanking us for an interesting lesson, so we didn't really mind.

The best fun came after school, though. We spent many happy hours playing games or football or just chatting with the children. On Friday afternoons, Lucy and I were in charge of sport, which had just been introduced at the school. Trying to organise fifty children into cricket teams is something I'll never forget. Another of my memories is playing in goal for a boys' football game. Even though Lucy and a group of little girls joined in as extra goalkeepers, we still managed to let the other side score!

I was terribly sad to leave. I felt I had learned as much as – if not more than – my pupils from the experience.

Part 4

Questions 21–25

Read the text and the questions below.
For each question, mark the correct letter **A**, **B**, **C** or **D** on your answer sheet.

Dream Job

Since 1969, Mark Harris has worked for a well-known toy manufacturer designing cars. When he started, he was the only man in the department, but now he is in charge of a team of 35 designers.

Mark first got interested in cars during his teens. His dad was a football coach and one day he took a car magazine away from one of his players during a practice session. He brought it home and gave it to Mark. From that moment on, cars became the love of Mark's life. He went on to study car design at university and then worked for a car company designing actual cars, before being persuaded by a friend to join the toy company and set up their design department.

Of all the cars he has designed, his favourite is the *Silver Sunrise*. It may not have achieved such high sales as some other cars, but it is important to Mark because it was the first time he was allowed to make a model that looked like a real car. 'Before that, the wheels on all the cars stuck out so they would go straight.' explained Mark. 'The *Silver Sunrise* was the first one where the wheels were under the body. It meant it didn't work so well on a race track but it looked amazing.'

Now in his 60s, Mark is approaching retirement. He finds it hard to imagine what that will be like. 'I have expensive hobbies, so it might be difficult to continue with them when I am no longer earning! Plus, I like coming in to work. Ideally I'd like to retire part time and work part time.'

21 In this text, the writer is

    A giving information about how to become a toy designer.

    B describing the career of one successful toy designer.

    C persuading people to consider a career as a toy designer.

    D saying what qualities are needed in a good toy designer.

22 Mark first became interested in cars

    A after reading about them.

    B while he was at university.

    C when his father began to talk about them.

    D by talking to someone from his football team.

23 Why does Mark like the *Silver Sunrise* so much?

   A It is his top-selling design.

   B It is very easy to play with.

   C It is the first toy car he ever designed.

   D It is more realistic than his earlier designs.

24 What does Mark say about retiring?

   A He has no plans to retire in the near future.

   B He would prefer not to give up work completely.

   C He is looking forward to taking up some new hobbies.

   D He has saved enough money to allow him to follow his interests.

25 What would Mark say about his job?

A
> It wasn't easy taking over such a big department as a young man, but I'll miss everyone when I leave.

B
> I'm proud of all the models I've designed. My only regret is that I never worked with real cars!

C
> My degree and previous work experience have been very helpful to me in my job. It's great to see how the design department has grown over the years.

D
> As soon as I saw the advertisement for this job I knew it was for me. Luckily the company agreed!

Part 5

Questions 26–35

Read the text below and choose the correct word for each space.
For each question, mark the correct letter **A**, **B**, **C** or **D** on your answer sheet.

Example:

0   **A**   get   **B**   find   **C**   make   **D**   take

Answer:

0	A B C D
	■ ☐ ☐ ☐

Robots

Robots can work in places humans can't easily **(0)** .... to. These include deep oceans, on **(26)** .... planets or on sites with bad pollution. Robots are also used in factories **(27)** .... they can work more quickly and accurately than a human, and **(28)** .... needing to rest.

Improvements in technology over the past 50 years have **(29)** .... that scientists are now able to create very clever robots. The most complicated of these can make **(30)** .... for themselves, learn new things, and **(31)** .... with problems. However, while robots **(32)** .... look like people are very common in science fiction films, they are very **(33)** .... in real life. Making a machine that can balance and move on two legs is a real **(34)** .... and is unnecessary for most of the jobs we need robots to do for us. However, a Japanese robot **(35)** .... as Asimo does walk on two legs and can even climb up and down stairs.

26	**A**	further	**B**	high	**C**	distant	**D**	long
27	**A**	unless	**B**	because	**C**	although	**D**	despite
28	**A**	without	**B**	before	**C**	until	**D**	after
29	**A**	intended	**B**	supposed	**C**	said	**D**	meant
30	**A**	results	**B**	decisions	**C**	thoughts	**D**	options
31	**A**	sort	**B**	manage	**C**	deal	**D**	handle
32	**A**	whose	**B**	that	**C**	what	**D**	where
33	**A**	rare	**B**	thin	**C**	little	**D**	narrow
34	**A**	difficult	**B**	trouble	**C**	fault	**D**	challenge
35	**A**	called	**B**	known	**C**	named	**D**	said

Writing

Part 1

Questions 1–5

Here are some sentences about a skiing holiday.
For each question, complete the second sentence so that it means the same as the first.
Use no more than three words.
Write only the missing words on your answer sheet.
You may use this page for any rough work.

Example:

0   It was Leah's first skiing holiday.

   Leah had never .... on a skiing holiday before.

Answer:

0	*been*

---

1   On Leah's first day, the ski slopes were covered with thick snow.

   On Leah's first day, thick snow .... the ski slopes.

2   It took Leah the whole morning to learn how to stop.

   Leah spent the whole morning .... how to stop.

3   Leah had lunch and then she tried the ski-lift.

   Leah didn't try the ski-lift .... she'd had lunch.

4   Leah often fell over, which she found annoying.

   Leah was .... because she fell over so often.

5   The instructor said the first three days would be the most difficult.

   The instructor said, 'The first three days .... the most difficult.'

Part 2

Question 6

You have arranged to go to the cinema with your English friend Charlie this evening, but you won't be able to go.

Write an email to Charlie. In your email, you should

- apologise to Charlie

- explain why you won't be able to go to the cinema

- suggest another activity that you can do together next week.

Write **35–45 words** on your answer sheet.

Part 3

Write an answer to **one** of the questions (**7** or **8**) in this part.
Write your answer in about **100 words** on your answer sheet.
Put the question number in the box at the top of your answer sheet.

Question 7

- This is part of a letter you receive from your English friend, Paul.

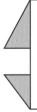

> I've saved enough money to buy a scooter.
> My parents say I should wait until I'm older
> and buy a car instead. Which do you think is
> better? What should I do?

- Now write a letter answering Paul's questions.

- Write your **letter** on your answer sheet.

Question 8

- Your English teacher has asked you to write a story.

- Your story must have the following title:

An important visitor

- Write your **story** on your answer sheet.

Listening Paper

01 [CD-ROM]

Part 1

Questions 1–7

There are seven questions in this part.
For each question there are three pictures and a short recording.
Choose the correct picture and put a tick (✔) in the box below it.

Example: Where is the boy's bag?

A ✔   B ☐   C ☐

---

1 What will Tracey do first?

A ☐   B ☐   C ☐

2 Which is the last film they will show this season?

  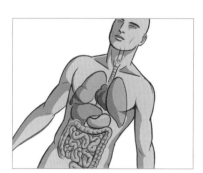

A ☐   B ☐   C ☐

3 Which photograph are they looking at?

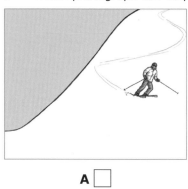  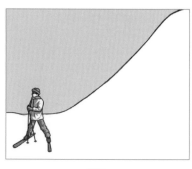

A ☐   B ☐   C ☐

4 Where is the art shop?

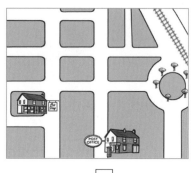 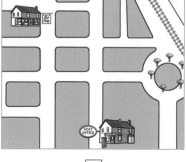 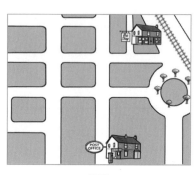

A ☐   B ☐   C ☐

5 How will the boy get home?

A ☐   B ☐   C ☐

6 Which jacket will the girl wear on the school trip?

A ☐

B ☐

C ☐

7 What was the worst thing about Julie's day at the theme park?

A ☐

B ☐

C ☐

02 [CD-ROM]

Part 2

Questions 8–13

You will hear a radio interview with a student, Amy Jones, who has just started her own business. For each question, put a tick (✔) in the correct box.

8	Amy Jones first began making jewellery when she	**A**	was a young child.	☐
		B	was at secondary school.	☐
		C	started university.	☐
9	Where can Amy's jewellery be bought?	**A**	in shops across the country	☐
		B	on the internet	☐
		C	in one local shop	☐
10	Amy decided against using her own name for her company because	**A**	it was rather boring.	☐
		B	it was difficult to spell.	☐
		C	it was hard to remember.	☐
11	How does Amy describe her jewellery?	**A**	Every design is different.	☐
		B	Some of the designs are very complicated.	☐
		C	Her designs have a modern appearance.	☐
12	What does Amy say about her life at the moment?	**A**	She would like to play less sport.	☐
		B	She is sometimes in trouble with her teachers.	☐
		C	She has very little free time.	☐
13	The next thing Amy plans to do is	**A**	research other possible careers in case this one fails.	☐
		B	give up university and concentrate on making jewellery.	☐
		C	move out of her parents' house as soon as possible.	☐

03 [CD-ROM]

Part 3

Questions 14–19

You will hear a woman talking on the radio about a mobile cinema.
For each question, fill in the missing information in the numbered space.

The Screen Machine

- The Screen Machine visits each location once every
  (14) .... weeks.

- The sides of the Screen Machine become the
  (15) .... of the cinema.

- Sometimes the motors in the Screen Machine need repairing because
  of damage from **(16)** ....

- Driving the Screen Machine onto the **(17)** ....
  can be difficult.

- Occasionally a film show has to be stopped because of
  (18) ....

- You can book seats beforehand from the **(19)** ....
  or by phone.

PRACTICE
TEST

 04 [CD-ROM]

Part 4

Questions 20–25

Look at the six sentences for this part.
You will hear a conversation between a boy, John, and a girl, Katie, about a birthday party.
Decide if each sentence is correct or incorrect.
If it is correct, put a tick (✔) in the box under **A** for **YES**. If it is not correct, put a tick (✔) in the box under **B** for **NO**.

		A YES	B NO
20	John is confident that his parents will let him have a party at home.	☐	☐
21	Last time John had a party he invited more people than he was supposed to.	☐	☐
22	John has asked his parents if he can have the party indoors.	☐	☐
23	Katie suggests finding out how the neighbours feel about the party.	☐	☐
24	Katie and John agree to have the party at Katie's house.	☐	☐
25	Katie offers to call Sonia about the music for the party.	☐	☐

Speaking Paper

Part 1

The examiner will ask you some questions about you, your life and your likes and dislikes.

For example:

1   What's your name?
2   Where are you from?
3   What is your favourite subject at school?
4   What do you usually do at the weekend?
5   Tell me about your family. Do you have any brothers or sisters?

Part 2

The examiner will describe a situation to you and give you a sheet of pictures. You will be given a specific task. You need to have a conversation with your partner to complete the task. Use the pictures to help you.

A friend of yours is going to stay with a British penfriend for the first time. Talk about the things your friend will need and decide what the most important things to take are.

Part 3

The examiner will give each of you a photograph on a similar theme, and ask you to talk about it for about a minute. You should describe the people in the picture, what they are doing, and the objects you can see.

Student A:

> This photograph shows someone relaxing. Show it to Candidate B. Please tell us what you can see in the photograph.

Look at photograph A opposite.

Student B:

> Your photo also shows someone relaxing. Show it to Candidate A. Say what you can see in the photograph.

Look at photograph B opposite.

Part 4

The examiner will ask you to have a discussion with your partner. You will be asked a question with the same topic as your photographs.

> Your photographs showed people relaxing. Now I'd like you to talk together about how important you think it is to rest and relax, and the things that you do to feel relaxed.

Part 3 • Photograph A

Part 3 • Photograph B

Exam answer sheets

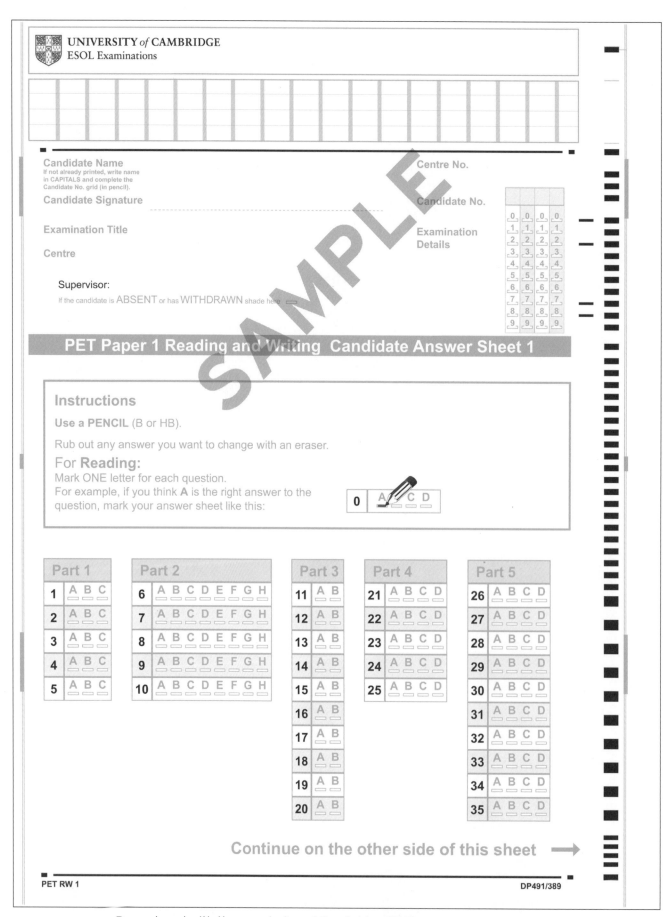

For **Writing (Parts 1 and 2):**

Write your answers clearly in the spaces provided.

Part 1: Write your answers below.		Do not write here
1		1 1 0
2		1 2 0
3		1 3 0
4		1 4 0
5		1 5 0

Part 2 (Question 6): Write your answer below.

Put your answer to Writing Part 3 on Answer Sheet 2 ⟶

Do not write below (Examiner use only).					
0	1	2	3	4	5

Reproduced with the permission of Cambridge ESOL.

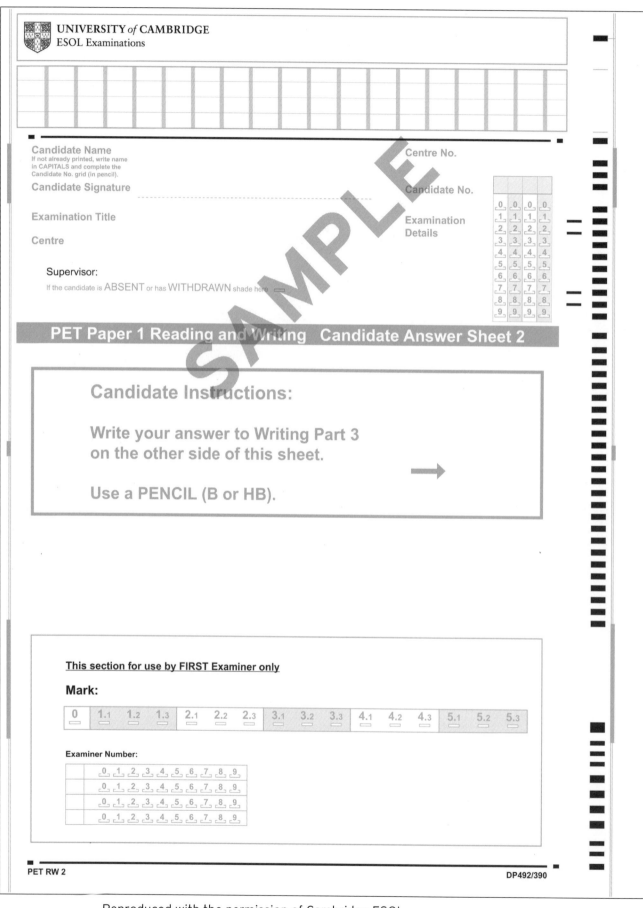

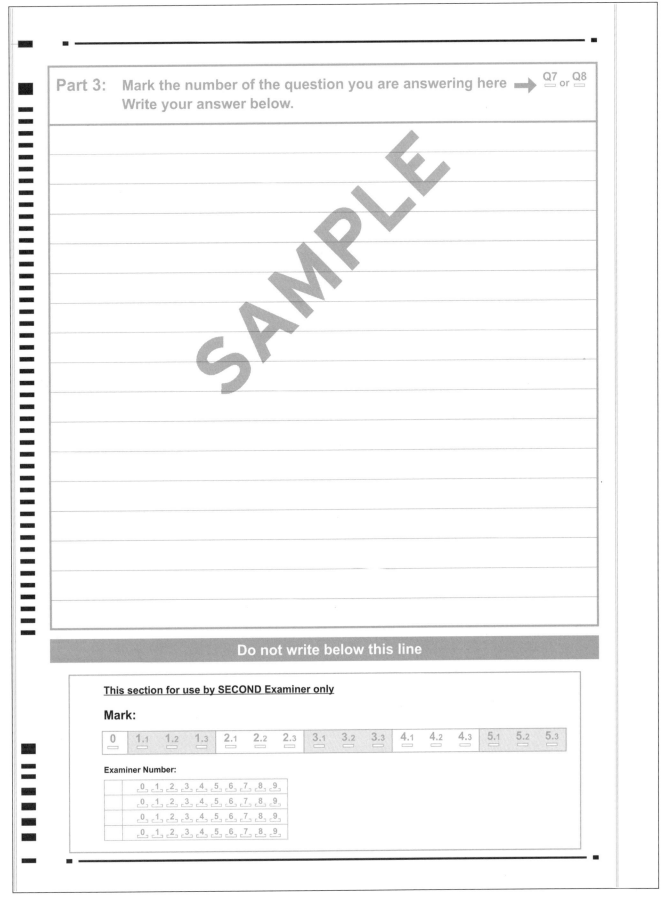

Part 3: Mark the number of the question you are answering here ➡ Q7 or Q8

Write your answer below.

Do not write below this line

This section for use by SECOND Examiner only

Mark:

| 0 | 1.1 | 1.2 | 1.3 | 2.1 | 2.2 | 2.3 | 3.1 | 3.2 | 3.3 | 4.1 | 4.2 | 4.3 | 5.1 | 5.2 | 5.3 |

Examiner Number:

	0 1 2 3 4 5 6 7 8 9
	0 1 2 3 4 5 6 7 8 9
	0 1 2 3 4 5 6 7 8 9
	0 1 2 3 4 5 6 7 8 9

Reproduced with the permission of Cambridge ESOL.

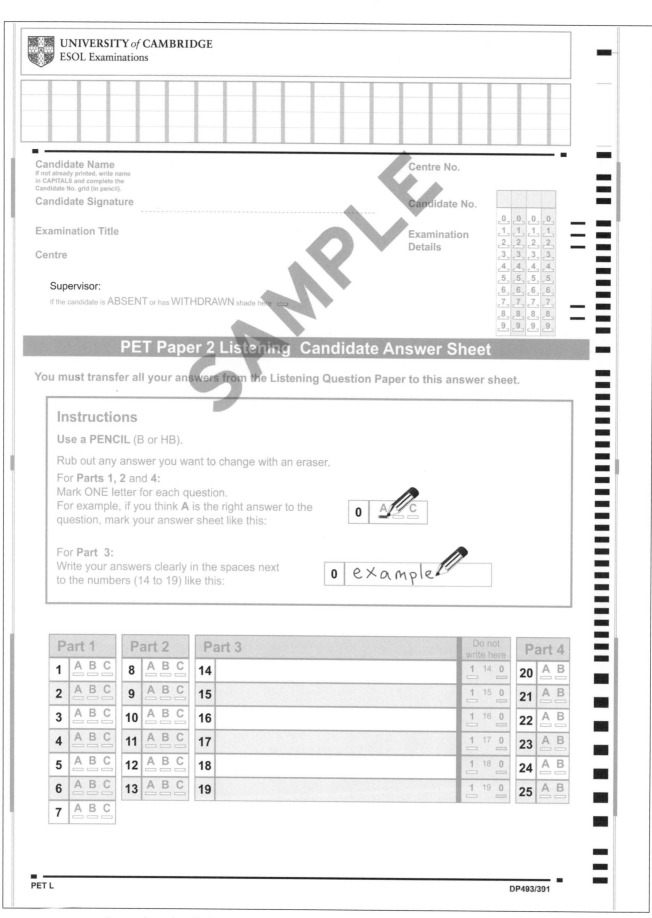

UNIVERSITY of CAMBRIDGE
ESOL Examinations

Candidate Name
If not already printed, write name
in CAPITALS and complete the
Candidate No. grid (in pencil).

Candidate Signature

Examination Title

Centre

Supervisor:

If the candidate is ABSENT or has WITHDRAWN shade here

Centre No.

Candidate No.

Examination Details

PET Paper 2 Listening Candidate Answer Sheet

You must transfer all your answers from the Listening Question Paper to this answer sheet.

Instructions

Use a PENCIL (B or HB).

Rub out any answer you want to change with an eraser.

For **Parts 1, 2** and **4:**
Mark ONE letter for each question.
For example, if you think **A** is the right answer to the
question, mark your answer sheet like this:

For **Part 3:**
Write your answers clearly in the spaces next
to the numbers (14 to 19) like this:

Part 1	Part 2	Part 3	Do not write here	Part 4
1 A B C	8 A B C	14	1 14 0	20 A B
2 A B C	9 A B C	15	1 15 0	21 A B
3 A B C	10 A B C	16	1 16 0	22 A B
4 A B C	11 A B C	17	1 17 0	23 A B
5 A B C	12 A B C	18	1 18 0	24 A B
6 A B C	13 A B C	19	1 19 0	25 A B
7 A B C				

PET L

DP493/391

Reproduced with the permission of Cambridge ESOL.

Irregular verbs

Infinitive	Past tense	Participle
be	was, were	been
become	became	become
begin	began	begun
bite	bit	bitten
break	broke	broken
bring	brought	brought
build	built	built
buy	bought	bought
catch	caught	caught
choose	chose	chosen
come	came	come
cost	cost	cost
do	did	done
dream	dreamt / dreamed	dreamt / dreamed
drink	drank	drunk
eat	ate	eaten
fall	fell	fallen
feel	felt	felt
fight	fought	fought
find	found	found
fly	flew	flown
forbid	forbade	forbidden
forget	forgot	forgotten
forgive	forgave	forgiven
get	got	got / gotten (US)
give	gave	given
go	went	gone
grow	grew	grown
have	had	had
hear	heard	heard
hide	hid	hidden
hit	hit	hit
hold	held	held
hurt	hurt	hurt
keep	kept	kept
know	knew	known
lead	led	led
learn	learnt / learned	learnt / learned
leave	left	left
let	let	let
light	lit / lighted	lit / lighted
lose	lost	lost
make	made	made
meet	met	met
pay	paid	paid
put	put	put

Infinitive	Past tense	Participle
read (/riːd/)	read (/red/)	read (/red/)
ride	rode	ridden
ring	rang	rung
rise	rose	risen
run	ran	run
say	said	said
see	saw	seen
sell	sold	sold
send	sent	sent
set	set	set
shake	shook	shaken
shoot	shot	shot
show	showed	shown / showed
shut	shut	shut
sing	sang	sung
sit	sat	sat
sleep	slept	slept
smell	smelt / smelled	smelt / smelled
speak	spoke	spoken
spend	spent	spent
spill	spilt / spilled	spilt / spilled
spread	spread	spread
stand	stood	stood
steal	stole	stolen
stick	stuck	stuck
stink	stank / stunk	stunk
strike	struck	struck
swear	swore	sworn
sweep	swept	swept
swell	swelled	swollen / swelled
swim	swam	swum
swing	swung	swung
take	took	taken
teach	taught	taught
tear	tore	torn
tell	told	told
think	thought	thought
throw	threw	thrown
understand	understood	understood
upset	upset	upset
wake	woke	woken
wear	wore	worn
weep	wept	wept
wet	wet / wetted	wet / wetted
win	won	won
write	wrote	written

Answer key

Unit 1
Lesson 1

1 1 E 2 A 3 B
4 F 5 D

2 1 photography
2 cycling
3 football
4 windsurfing
5 dancing
6 acting

3 1 album, camera, pictures
2 brakes, helmet, wheels
3 ball, goal, pitch
4 beach, board, sail
5 music, partner, steps
6 audience, curtain, stage

4 See you later.

5 1 Why aren't you speaking
to me?
2 Are you OK?
3 Please send me a message
before tonight.
4 Thanks for a great party.
5 Could you call me
tomorrow at 11?

Lesson 2

1 1 A 2 E 3 B
4 F 5 C

2 1 laptop
2 password
3 keyboard
4 screensaver
5 mouse mat

3 1 have
2 are eating
3 am using
4 needs
5 know

4 1 A 2 C

Unit 2
Lesson 1

1 1 very
2 absolutely, very
3 very, absolutely
4 very, absolutely

2 lazy / hard-working
mean / generous
polite /rude
sensible / silly
serious / funny
shy / confident
1 sensible
2 shy
3 funny
4 mean
5 polite

3 1 C   5 D   8 A
2 C   6 B   9 D
3 A   7 A   10 B
4 C

Lesson 2

1 1 fan
2 cushion
3 carpet
4 ceiling
5 mirror
6 curtains
7 cupboard
8 drawers
9 shelf
Word going down: furniture

2 1 so
2 too
3 enough
4 such
5 enough
6 so

Unit 3
Lesson 1

1 1 used to build
2 used to burn
3 used to make
4 used to hang
5 didn't use to have
6 used to store
7 didn't use to keep
8 used to eat

2 1 A 2 D 3 C 4 B

Lesson 2

1 1 cathedral
2 skyscraper
3 apartment block
4 museum
5 sculpture

2 1 due/owing to its position
on the coast
2 due/owing to flooding
3 Due/Owing to the heavy
traffic on the roads
4 Due/Owing to the singer's
illness

3 1 Traffic wasn't allowed to
come into the centre.
2 Food-sellers set up stalls in
the square.
3 A skating rink was built in
the park.
4 The streets were filled with
crowds of people of all
ages.
5 The event was enjoyed by
everyone who went there.
6 They will organise another
festival next year.

4 1 C 2 B 3 A 4 C

Answer key

Unit 4
Lesson 1

1
1 baked
2 spinach
3 vanilla
4 onion
5 grilled
6 dessert
Word going down: dinner

2
1 may / might
2 should
3 could
4 may / might
5 may / might

3
1 job
2 you help me
3 to plan
4 such a
5 more popular

Lesson 2

1 1 E   2 D   3 B   4 A

2
1 many
2 A couple of
3 some
4 a little
5 much

3 1 A   2 B   3 B   4 A
       5 B   6 A   7 B

Unit 5
Lesson 1

1
1 toes
2 shoulders
3 thumb
4 ankle
5 chin
6 throat
Word going down: stomach

2
1 sore
2 felt; eat
3 heavily; damage
4 medicine; hurt

3
1 You should hold it under cold running water for at least ten minutes. (A)
2 You ought to lie down quietly with your feet above your head for a few minutes. (D)
3 You should hold the soft part of your nose firmly for ten minutes. (B)

Lesson 2

1
1 amazing
2 frightening
3 bored
4 interesting
5 surprised
6 excited

2 1 E   2 C   3 A

Unit 6
Lesson 1

1
Reading across: board, fasten, miss, cabin, plane, helicopter
Reading down: platform, timetable, pilot, announcement

2
1 plane
2 cabin; fasten
3 pilot; helicopter
4 platform; announcement
5 miss; timetable

3
1 was waiting
2 phoned
3 missed
4 took
5 were flying
6 hit
7 felt
8 landed

Lesson 2

1 1 B   2 A   3 B   4 C

2
1 Everyone enjoyed themselves despite the wet weather.
2 Although we saw some beautiful parrots, we didn't find any monkeys.
3 We managed to climb to the top of the cliff in spite of our heavy bags.
4 I don't like snakes, although I'm glad they're protected.
5 We swam in the lake in spite of the freezing water.

3 1 B   5 A   8 C
       2 A   6 C   9 A
       3 C   7 D   10 D
       4 B

WORKBOOK

Answer key

Unit 7
Lesson 1

1 1 board
2 goal
3 pitch
4 track
5 helmet
6 athletics
Word going down: racket

2 1 more frequently
2 the best
3 more easily
4 the worst

3 1 B 2 A 3 B 4 B
5 A 6 A

Lesson 2

1 1 Since 4 Now
2 for 5 already
3 At first 6 yet

2 1 D 2 B 3 A 4 C

Unit 8
Lesson 1

1 1 can't
2 don't have to
3 have to
4 can't
5 don't have to
6 can
7 don't have to
8 can

2 Dear Margarita,
I enjoyed my English course, but there were lots of rules! We had to keep our rooms tidy and we couldn't move the furniture around. We didn't have to do our own laundry, luckily! We had to be on time for all meals and classes, and if we missed a class, then we couldn't go out in the evening. There were organised trips, but we didn't have to go on

those if we didn't want to! We could go to the library whenever we wanted and we didn't have to pay to use the computers, so I could check my emails whenever I wanted to!
Take care
Josephine

3 1 C 2 E 3 B

Lesson 2

1 1 That's the woman whose son is a pop star.
2 I live in the village where I was born.
3 I moved here in 2006 when I got this job.
4 The film that/which I saw last night starred Johnny Depp.

2 1 novelist
2 photographer
3 reporter
4 artist
5 scientist
6 manager
7 designer
8 sailor
9 interpreter
10 guitarist
11 footballer

3 1 D 5 B 8 A
2 B 6 D 9 C
3 C 7 A 10 B
4 A

Unit 9
Lesson 1

1 1 People will probably live for several hundred years.
2 There is unlikely to be any need for cash.
3 We may be able to download our memories onto a computer.

4 'Intelligent' robots might be the pets of the future.
5 We will travel around in driverless cars.

3 1 A 2 D 3 C

Lesson 2

1 1 I'm going to write to some politicians about global warming.
2 Are you going to recycle that bottle?
3 It isn't going to rain this afternoon.
4 Some parts of the world are going to have more droughts in the future.
5 I'm not going to leave the TV on standby anymore.
6 Is Mr Jones going to ask us to write a report about our visit to the exhibition?
7 There is going to be a storm tonight.
8 We aren't going to switch on the central heating.
9 Are tigers going to become extinct?
10 I am going to help clean up the beach on Saturday.

2 1 doesn't stop; will be
2 won't be able; stops
3 don't protect; will become
4 will meet; am
5 won't mark; give
6 will drive; are
7 count; can tell
8 rains; will die

4 1 foot
2 as/so much
3 use
4 has
5 unless

Answer key

Unit 10
Lesson 1

1 1 A 2 G 3 E
4 B 5 C 6 D

2 (sample answers)
1 If we stayed at the seaside, I'd be able to have fun on the beach.
2 If there were more kids on this campsite, we could organise a game of football.
3 If this campsite had a pool, I would go for a swim.
4 If Mum and Dad let me bring a friend, we could go out together in the evening.
5 If there were/was a town nearby, I could find some shops selling computer games.
6 If the weather were/was better, I wouldn't feel so miserable.

3 1 B 2 A 3 B 4 C

Lesson 2

1 1 discount
2 tent
3 guitar
4 audience

2 1 brought
2 recorded
3 taken
4 collected

3 1 should pack
2 can collect
3 must / have to carry
4 may use; should keep
5 can fill
6 must not set up

Unit 11
Lesson 1

1 1 similar; same
2 same
3 like
4 like
5 same

2 1 E a pair of strong leather waterproof boots
2 D a beautiful floor-length silk dress
3 B a pair of soft comfortable cotton pyjamas
4 A a new bright blue stripy swimming costume

3 1 B 5 B 8 C
2 C 6 A 9 C
3 D 7 B 10 D
4 A

Lesson 2

1 1 She needs to have/get her dress cleaned.
2 He needs to have/get his hair cut.
3 He needs to have/get his house painted.
4 She needs to have/get her eyes tested.

2 1 B 4 B 7 A
2 A 5 B 8 A
3 B 6 A 9 B

Unit 12
Lesson 1

1 1 looked, chose, had seen
2 had passed, offered
3 had been, got
4 got, had started

2 1 C 2 A 3 D

Lesson 2

1 1 Sam said (that) he had seen a strange light in the sky.
2 The reporter asked Sam to / if Sam could describe the light.
3 Sam said (that) it had been long and blue, and it had moved very fast.
4 The reporter asked (Sam) where the light had been.
5 Sam said (that) he had seen it / it had been over the clock tower and then it had disappeared in the direction of the castle.
6 The reporter said (that) it sounded like the Saturn Soldiers were back.

2 1 warned
2 suggested
3 told
4 explained
5 apologised

3 1 the age
2 didn't give
3 went
4 easy as
5 though

Answer key

Reading and Writing Paper

Reading

Part 1

1 B
2 B
3 A
4 C
5 A

Part 2

6 C
7 F
8 H
9 D
10 E

Part 3

11 B
12 A
13 B
14 B
15 A
16 B
17 A
18 B
19 A
20 B

Part 4

21 B
22 A
23 D
24 B
25 C

Part 5

26 C
27 B
28 A
29 D
30 B
31 C
32 B
33 A
34 D
35 B

Writing

Part 1

1 covered
2 learning
3 until
4 annoyed
5 will be / are

Part 2

(sample answer)

Hi Charlie

I'm really sorry but I shan't be able to go to the cinema with you this evening. I haven't finished my history essay yet and it's due in tomorrow.

How about going bowling one evening next week instead? Friday's best for me.

Tim

Part 3

Question 7

(sample answer)

Dear Paul

That's great that you can buy a scooter. You will have lots of fun on it. Perhaps your parents think a scooter is too dangerous. You should tell them that you will always wear a helmet and ride it carefully.

A car is very expensive. You must buy petrol and pay for repairs too. But a car is faster and more comfortable than a scooter, especially in the winter. Maybe when you have finished studying and have got a job you can buy a car, but not yet!

Write soon and tell me about your new scooter.

Sam

Question 8

(sample answer)

One day, when I was in junior school, our biology teacher told us a very important visitor was coming to our lesson. A man came in carrying lots of boxes. He put them on the table at the front. Then he started showing us the small creatures in the boxes and telling us about them. There were insects and spiders and mice and even a snake! We were allowed to hold some of them. At first we were nervous but soon everybody wanted to have turn.

I wasn't very interested in wildlife before but afterwards I decided that I that I would like to work in a zoo too, just like our important visitor.

Listening Paper

Part 1

1 C
2 A
3 B
4 B
5 C
6 A
7 B

Part 2

8 B
9 C
10 A
11 A
12 C
13 C

Part 3

14 seven
15 roof
16 salt / the sea air
17 ferry
18 strong winds
19 website

Part 4

20 B
21 A
22 B
23 A
24 B
25 B

Speaking Paper

Part 1

(sample answer)

(E=Examiner, C=Candidate)

E: Where are you from?

C: I'm from South Korea. I live in Seoul. I'm a high school student.

E: What is your favourite subject at school?

C: My favourite subject is geography. I like learning about other countries.

E: What do you usually do at the weekend?

C: I usually meet my friends in the city centre. We sometimes go to the cinema and then we go to a coffee shop afterwards.

E: Tell me about your family. Do you have any brothers or sisters?

C: There are four of us in my family - my parents and my twin brother and me. My father is a businessman and my mother is a hairdresser. My brother goes to the same school as me

Part 2

(sample answer)

A: Well I think he must remember to take his mobile phone so that he can talk to his friends.

B: That's a good idea, but maybe it won't work in England and it's very expensive to phone another country.

A: That's true. I think it's very important to take a present to his penfriend don't you.

B: Yes definitely. A box of chocolates or something like that.

A: Or a souvenir from his own country.

B: That's a good idea. What do you think about the camera?

A: It's good. He can take lots of pictures to show everyone when he gets home again.

B: And how about these clothes? They look very warm.

A: Yes well it's very cold in England so he'll need to take them. What about this book? It looks like a guidebook.

B: I'm not sure about that - it's not necessary. His penfriend can tell him everything about the places they visit.

A: OK. So what are the most important things to take? Maybe the camera.

B: I agree, and some warm clothes.

Part 2

(sample answer)

Candidate A

This girl is sitting on her bed and she's playing an electric guitar. She's looking at her laptop. I think there's some music on the screen. I think she's in her bedroom because I can see some photos and postcards on the wall behind her and some toy animals and a cushion. There are some cushions on the bed too - I can't remember the name but you put your head on them when you go to sleep. There are some stars on the wall too - it looks like a very nice bedroom. I think she is learning to play the guitar.

Candidate B

This man is watching a football match on television. He seems to be a football fan. I think it's a very exciting match because he's waving his arm. He's lying on the sofa. I think this is the living room because there is an armchair and a table with newspapers and magazines underneath it. He's got a drink in a glass on the table next to him. The man hasn't got any shoes on and he looks very relaxed.

Part 2

(sample answer)

A: Shall I start? I think its very important to relax because you can get too stressed if you don't relax. What do you think?

B: Yes, I think so too. You can even get ill if you don't relax enough. But what do you do to relax?

A: Well sometimes I go to my room and I lie down and listen to my favourite music and read a book. What about you? Do you like listening to music?

B: Oh yes. I listen to music all the time on my MP3 player. But if I want to relax I often watch television or play computer games.

A: I don't think computer games are relaxing - they can be so exciting and then it's difficult to stop playing.

B: Sometimes I play games until after midnight.

A: Really? I could never do that.

B: It's not a problem for me, it's good fun.

A: I like to take my dog for a long walk in the country or the park. That always makes me feel good because I forget my problems.

B: I haven't got a dog but I do like going out on my bicycle in the fresh air. It makes me feel more healthy. I think it's a good way to relax.

A: I agree with you.

CAMBRIDGE UNIVERSITY PRESS
www.cambridge.org/elt

RICHMOND PUBLISHING
www.richmondelt.com

© Richmond Publishing 2010
(PET *Direct* was originally published by Richmond
Publishing as *Target PET* © Richmond Publishing 2009)

Printed in China

ISBN 978-0-521-16711-6 Student's Book with CD-ROM
ISBN 978-0-521-16714-7 Workbook without answers
ISBN 978-0-521-16715-4 Workbook with answers
ISBN 978-0-521-16716-1 Teacher's Book with Class Audio CD
ISBN 978-0-521-16722-2 Student's Pack (*Student's Book with
CD-ROM and Workbook without answers*)

....

Acknowledgments:

Publisher: Deborah Tricker
Commissioning Editor: Matthew Duffy
Development Editor: Imogen Wyllie
Copy Editor: Sally Cooke
Proofreader: Sue Lightfoot
Design and Layout: Dave Kuzmicki
Cover Design: Georgie French
Photo Research: Magdalena Mayo
Audio Production:
Paul Ruben Productions, Inc. NYC
Legal consulting and copyright clearance:
Ruz Legal (Spain)

Publisher acknowledgements:
The publishers would like to thank the following
reviewers for their valuable feedback which has
made *Target KET for Schools* possible.

Gertrude Baxter (Universad Tecnologica de la Mixteca,
Mexico), Claudia Bonilla Cassani (Colegio del Tepeyac,
Mexico), Maria Consuelo Velasco (Colombia),
Karen Dyer (Madrid, Spain), Melissa Ferrin (Universad
Tecnologica de la Mixteca, Mexico),
Angieszka Gugnacka-Cook (ELC Łódź, Poland),
Andrea Harries (The English Company, Colombia),
Analía Kandel (Argentina), Helen Legge (Italy),
Gabby Maguire (International House Barcelona, Spain),
Laura Renart (ISP Dr Sáenz, Universad Virtual de
Quilmes, Argentina), Sarah Stats (International House,
Milan, Italy), Agnieszka Tyszkiewicz-Zora (ELC Łódź,
Poland)

The publishers would also like to thank all
those who have given their kind permission to
reproduce or adapt material for this book.

p. 16 "Adventure racing" © Realbuzz.com. All rights
reserved

*Every effort has been made to trace the holders
of copyright before publication. The publishers will
be pleased to rectify any error or omission at the
earliest opportunity.*

Illustrations:
Jason Ford, Scott Garrett, Aleix Pons Oliver,
Colin Shelbourn

Photographs:
I. Rovira; S. Enríquez; ACI AGENCIA DE FOTOGRAFÍA/
Alamy Images; CORDON PRESS/CORBIS/Gene Blevins/
La DailyNews, Brendan Regan; COVER/CORBIS;
DIGITALVISION; FOTONONSTOP; GETTY IMAGES
SALES SPAIN/Kent Mathews, Erik Isakson,
Daniel Allan, Alvis Upitis, Adrian Weinbrecht,
Johner Images, Alan Wycheck, Johannes Kroemer,
Charlotte Nation, Don Klumpp, Gregory Kramer,
Asia Images Group, Danny Martindale/FilmMagic,
Ghislain&Marie David de Lossy, Siri Stafford;
HIGHRES PRESS STOCK/AbleStock.com;
ISTOCKPHOTO; JOHN FOXX IMAGES; PHOTODISC;
STOCK PHOTOS; ProjectsAbroad; Rex Features;
SERIDEC PHOTOIMAGENES CD; ARCHIVO SANTILLANA